THE COLD WAR

FOR KIDS

CHARLES MCKINNEY

DR.HISTORY

The Cold War

THE COLD WAR

Chronicling the Most Significant Events from The Cold War

FOR KIDS

CHARLES MCKINNEY

DR. HISTORY

Don't Forget Your Free Bonus Downloads!

As our way of saying thank you, we've included in every purchase bonus gift downloads. If you've enjoyed reading this book, please consider leaving a review.

Or Scan Your Phone to open QR code

The Cold War:

Chronicling the Most Significant Events from The Cold War for Kids

Copyright © 2023 by Dr. History

TABLE OF CONTENTS

The Cold War

INTRODUCTION

"More than an end to war, we want an end to the beginnings of all wars."

- Franklin D. Roosevelt

After World War II, there was open but restrained competition and antagonism between the United States, the Soviet Union, and their respective allies. This was known as the Cold War. Why is there a need for us to learn about the Cold War? The Cold War, which occurred from the conclusion of the Second World War until 1990, was among the three most important events in history's second half. All of which had an impact on both the country and the world we are living in today.

According to one author, the Cold War was a stage in which the Soviet Union and the United States of America played principal roles. But what were some of the fundamental objectives, aspirations, prejudices, and worries on both sides that lay beneath the conflict's outward expressions? Most Americans, particularly President Roosevelt, firmly believed that America and Russia could work together to create a peaceful world.

On the other hand, the Soviet Union's leader, Joseph Stalin, wanted his supporters in the West to regard his demands as proper and reasonable. After all, Russia earned fair compensation since it had made a significant proportion of the sacrifices needed to overcome Germany. With an estimated 24 million fatalities, the U.S.S.R. suffered the most military and civilian losses during World War II while freeing sizable portions of Eastern Europe from Nazi rule. Stalin's post-war period objectives seem fair, if not downright harmless. However, there were issues with the strategy involved.

Despite the fact that the two countries were legally at peace, the time was marked by an expensive and destructive weapons competition and indirect wars fought in Asia, Latin America, and Africa. The two superpowers constantly aggravated each other using political scheming, military alliances, publicity, and economic assistance. America and the Soviet Union made significant investments in propaganda during the Cold War to sway public opinion, mainly through films.

The sections below will discuss the Cold War's origins and answer the questions above. The alliances formed among countries during the conflict will also be tackled. Further, we will also learn the significant historical events which, surprisingly, were consequences of the Cold War.

A photo of President Franklin D. Roosevelt in his hometown, Hyde Park, New York, in 1943. The Great Depression, World War II, and the start of the Cold War all occurred during his term in office.

AFTER WORLD WAR II

(From Left to Right) Picture of Joseph Stalin, Franklin Roosevelt, and Winston Churchill on the porch of the Russian Embassy. The photo was taken during the Tehran Conference in 1943.

There was tense cooperation between the United States, the Soviet Union, and Great Britain on the one hand and the latter on the other. However, it began to collapse after Nazi Germany surrendered in 1945, sparking the onset of the Cold War. Despite this, there was hardly any use of weapons on the front lines of the Cold War. It continued until 1991 and was primarily fought on political, industrial, and publicity fronts.

Alliances among nations dominated the Cold War. Franklin Roosevelt, Winston Churchill, and Joseph Stalin, collectively known as the "Big Three," guided the United States, United Kingdom, and Union of Soviet Socialist Republics (USSR), respectively, through World War II and right into the Cold War. Alliances during the Cold War outlined and amplified differences between democratic and socialist countries. They also increased the possibility that a conflict between two members could turn into a third world war.

The possibility of communist parties with Soviet influences gaining power in western Europe's democracies was a fear shared by the United States and the United Kingdom. Further, the Soviet Union's enduring control over eastern Europe was another concern. On the contrary, the Soviets were intent on keeping hold of eastern Europe to protect themselves from a potential return of German aggression. They were also determined to establish communism globally, mainly for ideological purposes.

As European countries allied with others to defend themselves against potential assault, the Cold War alliances started to take shape. Some thought this hostility might originate from a renewed Nazism, either as a concealed counterattack or terrorist rebellion against the occupation by the Allies. Adolf Hitler served as the head of the Nazi Party in Germany and is credited with founding the totalitarian movement known as Nazism. Others believed that a more significant danger came from the Soviet Union communist spies and freedom fighters.

In August 1945, the Soviet Union, the United States, and Great Britain had their final wartime summit. The destiny of Germany after the war was the most urgent matter at the Potsdam meeting. President Harry S. Truman of the United States, Winston Churchill of Great Britain, and Joseph Stalin of the Soviet Union served as representatives. It was Truman's first Big Three gathering at this time. The first two conferences—held in Tehran in 1943 and Yalta in 1945—were attended by President Franklin D. Roosevelt, who passed away in April 1945. However, the conference contributed to the onset of the Cold War because it did not resolve most of the very significant concerns.

In addition to wanting a united Germany, the Soviets insisted on Germany's complete demilitarization. Truman and many other American officials expressed grave concerns about the Soviet Union's European plans. Much of Eastern Europe was already under the control of the sizable Soviet army. The Big Three ultimately decided to partition Germany into three areas of occupation, one for each nation, and postpone talks of German reunification until later.

From the fall of 1945 through the beginning of 1947, the Council of Foreign Ministers hosted irregular but occasionally fruitful consultations between the two sides. Any attempt at the agreement was, however, hindered by mutual mistrust. Throughout the remainder of 1945 and 1946, Secretary of State James Byrnes often met with senior Soviet officials in an effort to negotiate a lasting, mutually agreed peace. The skeptical, self-absorbed Joseph Stalin, however, prevented his foreign minister from arriving at an agreement on the demilitarization of Germany and other concerns.

According to historian Robert Dallek, the postwar period would not be one of ongoing cooperation with the West but rather a new conflict between capitalism and communism. One that Stalin was ready to face by taking every opportunity he could. It has now become clear that Western attempts to settle essential disputes through diplomacy were ineffective due to Stalin's strict methods of thought and action.

Further, United States President Truman has his shortcomings as well. Roosevelt's confidence, public speaking ability, and familiarity with and expertise in international affairs needed to be improved. In private conversations and correspondence, Truman made crude remarks about other people that seemed to reflect his deep-seated self-doubt. For instance, he frequently called detractors `prima donnas" and stated the Russian diplomats at the Potsdam Conference were "pig-headed."

After World War II, there were also other severe concerns in East Asia. Further, many Americans were alarmed by the Soviet Union's post-World War II territorial expansion in Eastern Europe. However, the USSR grew resentful of American officials' hostile language, armament buildup, and meddling approach to world affairs. Despite the hostile environment, no single entity was solely responsible for the Cold War. Some historians even considered it unavoidable.

Fun Fact:

A journalist is credited with popularizing the name Cold War. In 1945, after the United States dropped atomic bombs on Hiroshima and Nagasaki, this phrase became widely used. Journalist George Orwell coined the term in an article that examined the significance of the atom bomb for international affairs. He claimed in his writing that the conflict with its neighbors led to a persistent state of the Cold War.

Fun Fact: *The First Cold War conflict.*

Iran-related tensions led to the first known Cold War crisis in March 1946. The Soviet Union supported a rebellion in northern Iran because the Iranian government declined to provide Russia with an oil privilege comparable to that granted to Britain. In addition, the Soviets were unwilling to withdraw their forces on March 2 in violation of a prior Big Three agreement.

Circle the Correct Word:

1. The tense cooperation between the United States, the Soviet Union, and Great Britain began to collapse after **Nazi Germany/Soviet Union** surrendered in 1945.

2. There was hardly any use of weapons on the front lines of the **World War II/Cold War.**

3. The **Nazis/Soviets** were intent on keeping hold of eastern Europe.

4. After World War II, other severe concerns arose in **East Asia/Southeast Asia**.

5. A **journalist/historian** is credited with popularizing the terminology for the Cold War.

Answers:

1. The tense cooperation between the United States, the Soviet Union, and Great Britain began to collapse after **Nazi Germany** surrendered in 1945.

2. There was hardly any use of weapons on the front lines of the **Cold War.**

3. The **Soviets** were intent on keeping hold of eastern Europe.

4. After World War II, other severe concerns arose in **East Asia.**

5. A **journalist** is credited with popularizing the terminology for the Cold War

THE SOVIET UNION

Robert Schuman, the foreign minister of France, helps ratify the North Atlantic Treaty. The image was taken in Washington, D.C., at a formal ceremony to establish the North Atlantic Treaty Organization (NATO) on April 4, 1949.

The previous northern Eurasian empire, known as the Soviet Union, or officially the Union of Soviet Socialist Republics (U.S.S.R.), spanned from the Baltic and Black seas to the Pacific Ocean. Fifteen Soviet Socialist Republics (S.S.R.) made up the Soviet Union in its final years: Azerbaijan, Armenia, Belarus, Georgia, Estonia, Kyrgyzstan, Kazakhstan, Lithuania, Latvia, Moldova, Russia, Turkmenistan, Tajikistan, Ukraine, and Uzbekistan. Moscow served as its capital, Russia's capital both then and now.

The Soviets (Councils) of People's Deputies laid the political groundwork for the U.S.S.R. The U.S.S.R.'s Supreme Soviet, based in Moscow, had official sovereignty over the whole Soviet Union. The first chamber of this organization, the Soviet of the Union, had 750 members chosen by single-member constituencies. Second is the Soviet of Nationalities, with 750 members comprising numerous political parties. The Union of Soviet Socialist Republics was, for the duration of its history, the largest nation with respect to land area. With more than 100 different ethnicities residing within its boundaries, it was among the most multicultural countries. The U.S.S.R. had the most extended coastal region in the world and the lengthiest borders.

The U.S.S.R. was established by a 1922 treaty between Russia, Ukraine, Belarus, and Transcaucasia (modern Armenia, Azerbaijan, and Georgia). The recently formed Communist Party, headed by Vladimir Lenin, a Marxist revolutionary, seized power. Fifteen Soviet Socialist Republics would make up the U.S.S.R. at its height. Upon Lenin's passing in 1924, the revolutionary Joseph Stalin, a Georgian-born man, ascended to power. Stalin turned the Soviet Union from an agricultural community into a military and industrial powerhouse during his rule, which lasted through his demise in 1953.

Millions of his own people died due to the tyrant's cruel policies, which were used to rule by intimidation. Stalin put into effect a number of Five-Year Plans to promote economic development and change in the Soviet Union. The rapid industrialization and regulation of agriculture were the main goals of the first Five-Year Plan. Later the Plan concentrated on arming and strengthening the military. Stalin terrorized Communist Party officials and the general public with his secret police to eradicate any potential opposition to his rule.

The Soviet Union and the United States battled as allies against the Axis powers in World War II. But there was tension in the alliance between the two countries. Nazi Germany, the Japanese Empire, and the Kingdom of Italy were the principal members of the Axis powers, a political union that sparked World War II. The Soviets despised the Americans for delaying their participation in World War II, which led to the destruction of millions of Russians. Moreover, the United States' unwillingness to recognize the U.S.S.R. as a lawful member of the global community caused the Soviets' resentment. These offenses grew into extensive mistrust and hostility between the two nations.

After World War II, there appears to have been a general sense of optimism for change throughout the nation. But there was a significant narrowing of political and ideological discipline at the end of 1945 and the start of 1946. These ideologies were created to isolate the nation's thinking from Western and democratic ideas or even from peaceful international cooperation. By 1948, the Soviet Union had imposed communist-leaning administrations in the nations of Eastern Europe that it had helped free from Nazi rule.

The political climate of the U.S.S.R., or more specifically, Stalin's environment, grew more anti-Semitic during the course of the postwar era. Anti-Semitism is the hatred of or prejudice against Jews as a religion or race. Anti-Semitism also continued in numerous other nations. Following the liberation of Auschwitz by his forces, Joseph Stalin's persecution of Jews continued until his demise in 1953.

Their fundamentally different beliefs influenced almost every aspect of how the United States and Russia approached internal and foreign issues. Personal freedoms guaranteed by the law, democracy, and capitalism were a principle held by most voters and U.S. government officials. Contrarily, Soviet leaders despised individual liberties and saw capitalism as obsolete and traditional ideas. The North Atlantic Treaty Organization was instituted in 1949 by Canada, the United States, and its European allies (NATO). A political display of power was being demonstrated against the U.S.S.R. and its allies by the Western bloc nations joining. Up to the collapse of the Soviet Union in 1991, the Cold War political conflict between the Eastern and Western blocs would continue in multiple forms on governmental, industrial, and media fronts.

Fun Fact:

The U.S.S.R. is seven times bigger than India. Between 1946 and 1991, when it was at its largest, the U.S.S.R. encompassed over 8,650,000 square miles (22,400,000 square kilometers), seven times the size of India and 2.5 times the size of the United States. The nation comprised almost one-sixth of the planet's land area, including approximately the northern third of Asia and Europe's eastern half.

Fun Fact:

IThe Soviet Union had an enormous army during the Cold War. In terms of the quantity and variety of weaponry they held, the Soviet Armed Forces were the greatest in the entire globe. By the 1980s, the U.S.S.R. had amassed an army and military weaponry superior to that of the U.S.

True or False:

1. The U.S.S.R.'s Supreme Soviet, based in Ukraine, had official sovereignty over the whole Soviet Union.

2. Lenin turned the Soviet Union from an agricultural community into a military and industrial powerhouse during his rule.

3. The Soviet Union and the United States battled as allies against the Axis powers in World War II.

4. The political climate of the U.S.S.R., or more specifically, Stalin's environment, grew more Semitic during the course of the postwar era.

5. By the 1980s, the U.S.S.R. had amassed an army and military weaponry superior to that of the U.S.

Answers:

1. The U.S.S.R.'s Supreme Soviet, based in Ukraine, had official sovereignty over the whole Soviet Union. **False. Based in Moscow.**

2. Lenin turned the Soviet Union from an agricultural community into a military and industrial powerhouse during his rule. **False. It was Stalin.**

3. The Soviet Union and the United States battled as allies against the Axis powers in World War II. **True**

4. The political climate of the U.S.S.R., or more specifically, Stalin's environment, grew more Semitic during the course of the postwar era. **False. Anti-Semitic political climate**

5. By the 1980s, the U.S.S.R. had amassed an army and military weaponry superior to that of the U.S. **True**

THE UNITED STATES AND THE MARSHALL PLAN

A photo of Joseph Stalin and his children. From the middle of the 20th century until his death in 1953, Joseph Stalin presided over the Soviet Union.

America had a reasonably open culture in which news media informed people even during conflict. The most important international topics are being debated in the political and media capitals of Washington and New York, respectively. During World War II, America, Britain, and Russia became well-known as the Grand Alliance. These allies' people, raw supplies, and manufacturing capabilities were more remarkable. But it was questioned whether America and Russia, the two powerhouses, would be able to work together to establish a sincere and long-lasting peace following the war. Before learning what transpired during the Cold War, let us first discover the alliances between the United States and other countries.

Communism was the primary threat facing the US during the Cold War. In a communist economy, the government owns the majority of the assets. Property often belongs to the people in a capitalist system like the United States. The US and the USSR faced off in the struggle for global dominance. Most American authorities concluded that the "containment" approach offered the best protection against Soviet unrest. According to diplomat George Kennan, the only option available to America was an abiding, persistent, but challenging, and attentive control of expansive Russian ambitions.

Scarcity, job losses, and disruption were widespread during the post-World War II era. The United States was concerned that these conditions would increase the influence of communist parties on citizens in western Europe. By 1947-1948, the Cold War had become more established when the Marshall Plan placed western Europe under American influence. Simultaneously, the Soviet Union had founded outwardly communist regimes in eastern Europe. The Marshall Plan was a United States-supported initiative that aimed to revive the economy of 17 western and southern European nations. The program would help democratic institutions endure after World War II.

George C. Marshall, the then-US Secretary of State, proposed funding a European self-enabling initiative. Under the Marshall Plan, nearly all European nations initially received support. Still, some decided to withdraw under the authority of the Soviet Union. The countries that stayed were: Western Germany, Denmark, Austria, France, Belgium, Iceland, Greece, Ireland, Italy, the Netherlands, Luxembourg, Norway, Sweden, Portugal, Switzerland, Turkey, and the United Kingdom. The program was officially known as the European Recovery Program and was successfully implemented from April 1948 to December 1951. The western European nations engaged had a

15–25% increase in their gross domestic products during this time.

The Soviet tyrant implemented policies that, in his opinion, restrained the West, condemning the Truman Doctrine and the Marshall Plan as capitalist offensive operations against his government. President Harry S. Truman founded the Truman Doctrine. It stated that the United States would grant diplomatic, armed services, and economic assistance to any democratic country under attack from internal or external dictatorial forces. In May 1947, the democratic, noncommunist leader of Hungary, Ferenc Nagy, was forced from power. The Cominform was created in September 1947 to strengthen Moscow's grip over the global communist movement. It included the Communist Parties of France, Italy, and six East European countries. Additionally, in February 1948, Soviet allies ousted the democratically elected Czechoslovak administration.

Almost at the same time, From June 1948 to May 1949, the Berlin Blockade, ordered by Joseph Stalin, barred all road and waterways traffic between West Berlin and West Germany.

Stalin reportedly thought the blockade would drive the West to discuss a resolution to the German concern with Russia. He allegedly feared a powerful and rebuilt West Germany more than anything else. The Berlin Blockade, one of the first significant global crises of the Cold War era, revealed the profound ideological gaps that separated East and West. In response, the Western Allies launched a sizable airlift to support West Berlin.

Despite continually strained relations, neither side desired conflict. Stalin maintained open lines of communication, and Truman refrained from pressing the western surface right of access to Berlin. After unsuccessful talks in Moscow throughout the summer, Washington was inclined to give up on talks with Russia. Further, this led to organizing a formal western defense pact, which became the North Atlantic Treaty Organization (NATO) in April 1949. A West German state was also founded, governed by the passionately anti-communist Konrad Adenauer.

Many Americans believed that Truman realized the high aspirations of Woodrow Wilson and Franklin Roosevelt, much as Stalin was presumably walking in Hitler's footsteps. Even many Americans who disagreed with Truman's policies nevertheless saw the United States as the world's moral leader. Truman believed that America had a special and honorable destiny. Though with reluctance, many West Europeans, appreciative of American support in the fight against the Nazis and rehabilitation after the war, embraced this notion. However, it was clear that Moscow felt differently.

Fun Fact: *Distribution of $13 billion worth of financial assistance.*

A mainly established department called the Economic Cooperation Administration (ECA) dispensed over $13 billion in financial help within four years. It was utilized in assisting with the restoration of industrial and agricultural productivity, the establishment of economic security, and the growth of trade. The help was primarily provided through outright payments, with loans making up the rest.

Fun Fact: *Trillions of dollars were spent by the United States.*

US military expenditures totaled an estimated $8 trillion throughout the Cold War. The financial cost of the conflict and the number of Soviet fatalities has proven challenging to measure. Economists and scholars think it goes beyond the United States. Nations raised their national debts and taxes to cover their wartime expenditures.

Questions:

1. During World War II, which countries were collectively known as the "Grand Alliance?" Why were they called such?

2. What were the three widespread conditions after World War II?

3. Why did Stalin order the construction of the Berlin Wall (Berlin Blockade)?

4. What was the western defense pact organized after an unsuccessful talk with the Soviets in Moscow?

5. What is the Marshall Plan? Was it successful?

Answers:

1. During World War II, which countries were collectively known as the "Grand Alliance?" Why were they called such? **Britain, America, and Russia. These allies' people, raw supplies, and manufacturing capabilities were more remarkable.**

2. What were the three widespread conditions after World War II? **Scarcity, Job losses, and Disruption**

3. Why did Stalin order the construction of the Berlin Wall (Berlin Blockade)? **Stalin reportedly thought the blockade would drive the West to discuss a resolution to the German concern with Russia.**

4. What was the western defense pact organized after an unsuccessful talk with the Soviets in Moscow? **The North Atlantic Treaty Organization (NATO)**

5. What is the Marshall Plan? Was it successful? **The Marshall Plan was a program to fund a European self-enabling initiative. Under the Marshall Plan, nearly all European nations initially received support. Yes, it was successful, with a 15–25% increase in the gross domestic product of the nations involved.**

The Cold War

NORTH ATLANTIC TREATY ORGANIZATION (NATO) AND THE WARSAW PACT FORMATION

The Soviet Union leader, Nikita Khrushchev, with U.S. President John F. Kennedy in Vienna, in 1961. Khrushchev successfully mediated talks with the US to ease Cold War hostility.

The North Atlantic Treaty Organization (NATO) has been mentioned a few times in the previous sections. Let us learn what NATO is and its purpose. The founding of NATO sparked expectations for peace, unity, and common values during a time of disorder, disaster, and hopelessness. It is important to remember that Western Europe, not the United States, took the lead in creating NATO.

World War II in Europe was declared over in May 1945. The hard-won triumph left the continent in ruins and exposed to an increasing threat of Soviet occupation. Without launching a shot, Russia has taken up eight European nations. The United States and Great Britain objected, claiming that Russia had breached her pact and that the threat of aggression had persuaded these nations. However, Russia disregarded the objections. Communists challenged democratic governments around Europe with assistance from the Soviet Union. The democratically elected administration of Czechoslovakia was overthrown in February 1948 by the Communist Party with covert aid from the Soviet Union.

Beginning in 1948, the Cold War was at its height. During this time, the Soviet Union attempted to blockade the parts of West Berlin controlled by the West but failed. The Soviet Union blasted its first nuclear weapon in 1949, breaking America's hold on the atomic bomb. Additionally, the same year saw the rise to prominence of the Chinese communists in mainland China.

On April 4, 1949, Belgium, France, the Netherlands,

Luxembourg, the United Kingdom, Denmark, Norway, Portugal, Italy, Canada, Iceland, and the United States joined the North Atlantic Treaty. They pledged to stand together against violence. An assault on one would be an assault on everyone. The North Atlantic Treaty Organization, commonly abbreviated as NATO, was created by these 12 countries.

It is only partially accurate that the North Atlantic Treaty Organization was established in reaction to the Soviet Union's aggression. The development of the Alliance was a component of a larger plan to accomplish three goals. The first involved preventing Soviet expansion, and the second was preventing the reemergence of nationalist hostility in Europe by maintaining a significant North American representation. Thirdly, NATO was established to promote political union in Europe.

In 1950, the North Korean communist regime, backed by the Soviet Union, invaded South Korea, which the United States supported. This conflict dragged on unresolved until 1953. Cold War hostilities mostly subsided between 1953 and 1957 due to the passing of longstanding Soviet ruler Joseph Stalin in 1953.

However, the collision continued. Nikita Khrushchev rose to power after Stalin's death.

In 1955, West Germany was accepted to the North Atlantic Treaty Organization by Western nations. This led to the Soviet Union creating the Warsaw Pact union in eastern and central Europe that same year. Officially known as the Warsaw Treaty of Friendship, Cooperation, and Mutual Assistance, the Warsaw Pact was created on May 14, 1955. Albania, Bulgaria, East Germany, Czechoslovakia, Romania, Hungary, and the Soviet Union made up its initial members.

After taking office at the beginning of 1955, Soviet leaders Nikita Khrushchev and Nikolay Bulganin embarked on a strategy to reinforce Soviet control over their territories. The Warsaw Pact was the initial step in that agenda. The Warsaw Pact granted the Soviet Union a centralized military leadership and the means to strengthen its grip on the other signatory nations steadily.

Fun Fact:

The United States and the Soviet Union battled for control of as many nations as possible throughout the 40-year-long Cold War. It was a power struggle. Despite the conclusion of the Cold War, which resulted in the Soviet Union's disintegration and collapse in 1991, it continues to impact global politics today.

Fun Fact:

During the Cold War, a teen piloted an aircraft and landed it on a bridge. German pilot Mathias Rust, then 18 years old, made headlines when he memorably made an emergency landing in Moscow on May 28, 1987, not far from Red Square. From Helsinki, Finland, he took a plane to Moscow. Upon his arrest, Rust claimed that it was his effort to terminate the conflict. The aircraft served as a symbolic link between the east and west.

Fill In the Blanks to Complete the Story

The founding of _________ sparked expectations for peace, unity, and common values during a time of disorder, disaster, and hopelessness. World War II in Europe was declared over in May _______. The hard-won triumph left the continent in ruins and exposed to an increasing threat of ___________ occupation.

Beginning in 1948, the _________ was at its height. Additionally, the same year saw the rise to prominence of the _________________ in mainland China. The North Atlantic Treaty Organization, commonly abbreviated as NATO, was created by these 12 countries. They pledged to stand together against _______________.

Answer:

The founding of **NATO** sparked expectations for peace, unity, and common values during a time of disorder, disaster, and hopelessness. World War II in Europe was declared over in May **1945**. The hard-won triumph left the continent in ruins and exposed to an increasing threat of **Soviet** occupation.

Beginning in 1948, the **Cold War** was at its height. Additionally, the same year saw the rise to prominence of the **Chinese communists** in mainland China. The North Atlantic Treaty Organization, commonly abbreviated as NATO, was created by these 12 countries. They pledged to stand together against **violence.**

MISSILE CRISIS

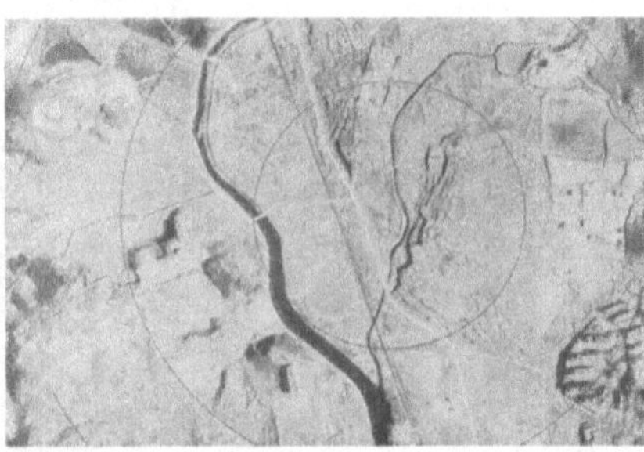

Aerial photos of Nagasaki, Japan before (left) and after the (right) bombing in August 1945. The bombings at Hiroshima and Nagasaki prompted Japan's surrender.

The Cold War saw several significant concerns, including the atomic energy strategy. For the duration of the conflict, America and Britain collaborated closely to create nuclear weapons. Roosevelt opted not to inform the Soviets about the proposal. Although it was only after the first bomb had been detonated in New Mexico that Truman brought up the new weapon during a brief conversation with Stalin in Potsdam in July 1945.

The Cold War environment has grown more intense, and the issues around atomic energy were extremely complicated. Because of this, it was highly improbable that America and Russia could have reached an understanding of global control of nuclear technology in 1946 and avoided an atomic arms rivalry. However, despite its flaws, the Truman regime made an attempt in that direction.

A photo of Hiroshima, Japan which was completely destroyed by the atomic bomb on August 6, 1945, at precisely 8:15 a.m. The Hiroshima Prefectural Industrial Promotion Hall is the structure that is still partly surviving.

Hiroshima and Nagasaki, two Japanese cities, were successfully bombed in August 1945, ending the Pacific War and forcing Japan to surrender. It seemed justified for America to employ nuclear warheads. According to Averell Harriman, the U.S. ambassador in Moscow, these events must have unexpectedly rekindled the Soviets' sense of uneasiness. A suggestion was made to create a worldwide "Atomic Development Authority" to oversee all facets of nuclear energy. The idea was reasonable, at least from the U.S. perspective. However, the Soviets would have probably rejected it due to Stalin's goal to give his country nuclear weapons to achieve military parity with America. Thus, both countries kept up their extensive nuclear efforts, which resulted in the initial successful Soviet tests in 1949 and the beginning of the 1950s.

The years 1958–1962 saw the Cold War at another critical point. The two countries collaborated to build intercontinental ballistic missiles (ICBM) or guided missiles. However, the Soviet Union began covertly deploying missiles in Cuba that might be used to conduct nuclear assaults on American cities. A ballistic missile is a kind of missile that launches warheads at a landing point using projectile motion. These weapon systems are only activated for short periods—most of the flight is non-powered. While ICBMs are released on a sub-orbital flight, short-range ballistic missiles remain in the Earth's atmosphere. The reach of an ICBM exceeds 5,500 kilometers.

The Cuban missile crisis, which broke in 1962 over Soviet nuclear-armed cruise missiles stationed in Cuba, was a significant conflict that nearly resulted in war between the U.S. and the U.S.S.R. The Soviet leader Nikita Khrushchev had pledged in May 1960 to protect Cuba with Soviet weapons. Further, he presumed that the United States would not take any action to stop the placement of Soviet medium- and intermediate-range ballistic Cuban missiles. If fired from Cuba, such weapons could swiftly strike a significant portion of the eastern United States.

The United States carefully examined its choices of a prompt Cuban invasion (or air raids of the missile bases), a siege of the island, or more diplomatic maneuvering. U.S. President John F. Kennedy decided to impose a naval "quarantine" or restriction on Cuba to stop further Soviet missile supplies. On October 22, Kennedy declared a quarantine and warned that American forces would confiscate any "offensive weapons and associated equipment" that Soviet warships could try to ship to Cuba. In the days that followed, Soviet ships headed for Cuba changed their course to avoid the quarantined area.

Khrushchev submitted on October 28, notifying Kennedy that construction on the missile bases would stop and that the weapons already in Cuba would be sent back to the Soviet Union. Kennedy pledged that the U.S. would never invade Cuba in exchange.

Fun Fact:

Images Captured from A U-2. A U.S. aircraft used for conducting surveillance was the Lockheed U-2. The U.S. prohibited U-2 flights over Cuban territory in September 1962 out of concern that Cuba would fire down a CIA-operated U-2. On October 14, a U-2 mission led by Major Richard S. Heyser flew over Cuba and captured images while passing at a high elevation. The medium- and intermediate-range ballistic missile installations were seen in the photographs.

Fun Fact:

A book was written by Robert F. Kennedy, President Kennedy's brother, titled Thirteen Days. The Cuban Missile Crisis lasted thirteen days between when John Kennedy learned about the issue, and Nikita Khrushchev declared on Radio Moscow that the missiles would be removed. Robert F. Kennedy wrote a book that detailed the situation. Later, it was transformed into the same-titled 2000 movie.

Match the Year and Events:

Can you match the year with the events?

1958–1962	Hiroshima and Nagasaki bombing
1962	A brief conversation between Truman and Stalin in Potsdam
1949–1950	Cuban Missile Crisis
July 1945	successful Soviet nuclear weapons tests
August 1945	Collaboration to build intercontinental ballistic missiles (ICBM)

Answers:

Can you match the year with the events?

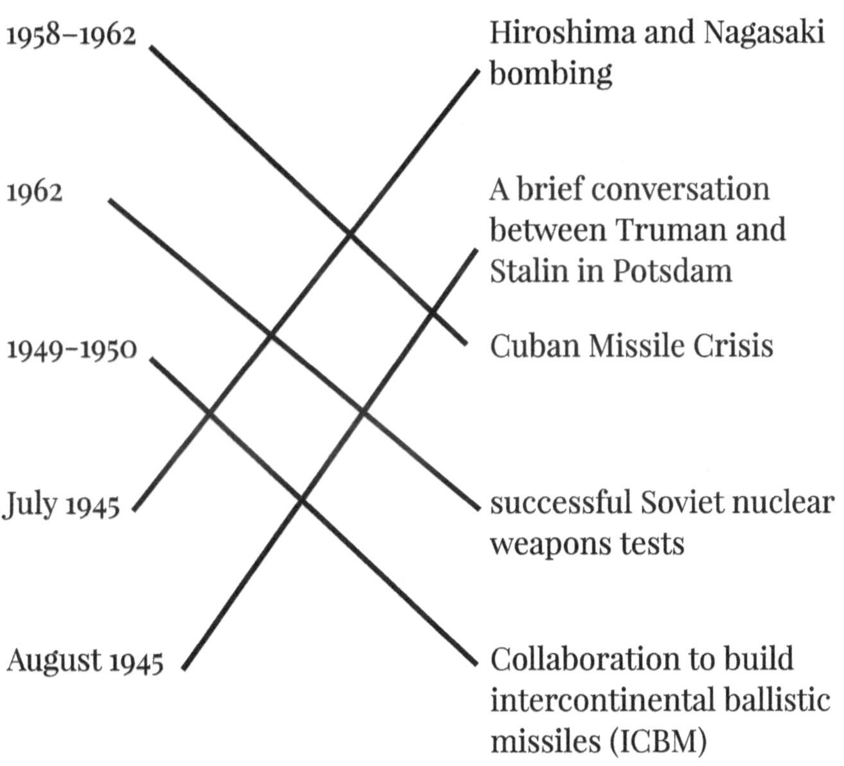

BANS ON NUCLEAR TESTING AND RESTRICTIONS ON THE PRODUCTION OF STRATEGIC MISSILES

The U.S.-Soviet relationship reached its most hostile point during the Cuban missile crisis. The incident also represented the world's closest encounter with nuclear war in history. On August 5, 1963, the Soviet Union, the U.S., and the U.K. signed the Nuclear Test-Ban Treaty, officially known as the "Treaty Banning Nuclear Weapons Tests in the Atmosphere, in Outer Space, and Under Water," in Moscow. The treaty prohibited all nuclear weapon tests other than those carried out underground. The agreement does not call for control stations, on-site assessments, or an international oversight organization. It did not limit the use of nuclear weapons during times of war, stop their manufacturing, or diminish atomic stockpiles.

The harm caused by atmospheric radioactive contamination

caused by nuclear weapons testing above ground was the driving force for the creation of the pact. By 1955, this issue had elevated to a significant national concern. During that period, the Soviet Union and the United States, the two leading nuclear powers, issued several suggestions and counter-suggestions on the prohibition of nuclear tests. The United States and the Soviet Union momentarily halted their testing for most of 1959. Still, talks over the following two years were hindered by rekindled Cold War conflicts between the two nations.

The Cuban missile crisis, which clearly exposed the risks of nuclear conflict, hastened the eventual reconciliation of the U.S. and the U.S.S.R. More than 100 other entities signed the agreement in the months following its first approval by the three founding parties in August 1963, except France and China. Talks on the Comprehensive Nuclear Test Ban Treaty, which would have prohibited nuclear tests below ground, did not start until 1977. The U.S., U.K., and the U.S.S.R. had signed a convention the year before forbidding the use of nuclear weapons for "peaceful" purposes, or what is known as nuclear explosions allegedly carried out for civil engineering works.

Apart from nuclear testing agreements, the U.S. and the U.S.S.R. discussed their aim to limit the production of strategic nuclear weapons missiles. Formally known as Strategic Arms Limitation Talks (SALT), the Soviet Union and the U.S. inked the first pacts, known as SALT I and SALT II, in 1972 and 1979, respectively. These agreements were designed to halt the nuclear-armed rivalry in strategic (long-range or intercontinental) ballistic missiles.

The Treaty on Anti-Ballistic Missiles (A.B.M.) Systems and the Interim Agreement and Protocol on Limitation of Strategic Offensive Weapons were the two most significant pacts in the ensuing agreements (SALT I). On May 26, 1972, during a conference held in Moscow, both documents were signed by President Richard M. Nixon on behalf of the United States and Leonid Brezhnev, general secretary of the Soviet Communist Party.

Anti-ballistic missiles that could hypothetically be used to shoot down approaching intercontinental ballistic missiles (ICBMs) released by the opposing superpower were governed under the A.B.M. Treaty. Each party was only allowed 100 interceptor missiles and one A.B.M. deployment zone under the treaty's terms. The United States Senate approved the A.B.M. pact on August 3, 1972.

Late in 1972, the SALT II talks began, lasting for seven years. As it was ultimately negotiated, the SALT II pact placed restrictions on the number of strategic weapons. For instance, missiles can be fitted with numerous independently targetable reentry vehicles (MIRVs). Its goal was to postpone the moment when the land-based ICBM systems of both sides would be exposed to an attack from these missiles. The pact imposed a maximum of 2,400 such weapon systems on both sides. On June 18, 1979, President Jimmy Carter and Brezhnev formally ratified the SALT II agreement in Vienna.

In January 1980, following the Soviet invasion of Afghanistan, Carter decided to withdraw the treaty from Senate consideration due to escalating tensions between the world powers. However, in the following years, the U.S. and the U.S.S.R. voluntarily complied with the SALT II weapons reduction.

Fun Fact: *The Shoelace Code.*

The US devised its low-tech methods for gathering intelligence. The Central Intelligence Agency (CIA) created a complicated code depending on how their shoes were tied. It allowed its secret agents and sources to deliver messages in various ways. The designs on the shoelaces could mean "I have info," "Follow me," or "I have another person with me."

Fun Fact: "*In God We Trust.***"**

Congress incorporated the words "under God" into the Pledge of Allegiance during the Cold War to further the idea that the Soviets were atheists. In the 1970s, the US released tens of thousands of bibles into Romania as part of its anti-atheist efforts.

Match Phrases:

Phrases:

- An agreement prohibiting all nuclear weapon tests
- An agreement that limits the production of nuclear weapon missiles
- A treaty governing the use of intercontinental ballistic missiles (ICBMs)
- A pact that placed restrictions on the number of strategic weapons owned

Answers:

- SALT I
- SALT II
- Treaty on Anti-ballistic Missiles (ABM)
- Nuclear Test Ban Treaty,
- Strategic Arms Limitation Talks

Answers:

- An agreement prohibiting all nuclear weapon tests **(Nuclear Test Ban Treaty)**
- An agreement that limits the production of nuclear weapon missiles **(SALT I)**
- A treaty governing the use of intercontinental ballistic missiles (ICBMs) **[Treaty on Anti-ballistic Missiles (ABM)]**
- A pact that placed restrictions on the number of strategic weapons owned **(SALT II)**

DEMOCRACY ON THE RISE

Mikhail Gorbachev was the final ruler of the U.S.S.R. He introduced economic transformation that destroyed institutions that depended on nationalized commodities and opened his nation to the West.

America and The Soviets avoided outright military conflict in Europe for the duration of the Cold War. Nevertheless, they only participated in actual military operations to prevent allies from switching sides or to topple them once they had. Thus, in order to maintain communist authority in Hungary, East Germany, Czechoslovakia, and Afghanistan, the Soviet Union dispatched troops there. On the other hand, the United States sponsored a failed Cuban invasion in 1961, overthrew a leftist party in Guatemala, and occupied Grenada and the Dominican Republic. Additionally, the U.S. made a prolonged (1964–1975) and fruitless attempt to stop communist North Vietnam from annexing South Vietnam.

However, during the 1960s and 1970s, the fluctuating conflict between the Soviet and American alliances gave way to a more complex pattern of global relations. The globe was no longer divided into two distinctly opposed political factions. In 1960, there was a significant rift between the Soviet Union and China that grew over time. The communist alliance's solidarity was fractured. While this was happening, western Europe and Japan saw strong economic growth through the 1950s and 1960s, which helped them gain ground with the United States in relative strength. Less powerful nations had more freedom to establish their independence and frequently demonstrated resistance to force or persuasion from powerful countries.

There was a brief period of heightened Cold War tensions in the early 1980s. It was when the two great powers fought for dominance in the Third World and pursued their tremendous arms development. But in the late 1980s, under Mikhail S. Gorbachev's Soviet Union leadership, the Cold War started to disintegrate. Mikhail Gorbachev was a senior Communist Party official who assumed office in 1985. A failing political system and a stagnating economy were what he inherited.

Gorbachev started work on smoothing the Soviet political structure. He eliminated the dictatorial elements of the Soviet system. Moreover, Gorbachev consented to the downfall of communist governments in the Soviet-alliance nations of eastern Europe in 1989–1990. Czechoslovakia, East Germany, Hungary, and Poland all welcomed democratic regimes. The integration of West and East Germany under NATO's guidance, again with Soviet consent, came swiftly after.

Another significant factor in the Cold War disintegration was U.S. President Richard Nixon. Shortly after taking office, President Nixon began applying a new foreign relations method. He proposed that, rather than seeing the globe as an antagonistic, "bipolar" state, more sides may be created by diplomacy rather than force. The president pushed for the U.N. to acknowledge the communist regime in China. Further, he built diplomatic ties with Beijing after visiting the city in 1972. Simultaneously, Nixon implemented a policy of "relaxation" concerning the Soviet Union.

The Cold War flared up again under President Ronald Reagan despite Nixon's endeavors. Like many other politicians of his era, he thought that the growth of communism threatened democracy everywhere. He, therefore, worked to support anticommunist regimes and uprisings worldwide with money and weapons. Reagan was fighting communism in Central America, but the Soviet Union was falling apart at the same time.

Fun Fact: *Third World Countries.*

During the Cold War, the phrase "Third World country" had a very different connotation. It was used to describe nations that remained neutral during the conflict. Europe, the U.S., and its supporters were regarded as the first world. In contrast, the U.S.S.R. and its collaborators were referred to as the second world. The phrase is now used to describe the least advanced countries in the global south.

Fun Fact: *Proxy Battles.*

The Soviet Union and the United States backed several proxy wars worldwide for more than forty years during the Cold War. The superpowers supported opposing forces or engaged in direct combat with communist or capitalist groups in the Korean War, Vietnam War, and other armed engagements.

Complete the Sentence:

1. America and The Soviets avoided outright military conflict in _ _ _ _ _ for the duration of the Cold War.

A. China   B. Moscow   C. Europe

2. The U.S. made a prolonged (1964–1975) and fruitless attempt to stop communist _ _ _ _ _ _ from annexing South Vietnam.

A. Russia   B. North Vietnam   C. China

3. But in the late 1980s, under _ _ _ _ _ _ _ _ _'s leadership, the Cold War started to disintegrate.

A. Mikhail S. Gorbachev   B. Franklin D. Roosevelt   C. Nikita Khrushchev

4. Another significant factor in the Cold War disintegration was U.S. President _ _ _ _ _ _ _ _ _.

A. Franklin Roosevelt   B. Richard Nixon   C. Harry Truman

5. The Soviet Union and the United States backed several _ _ _ _ _ _ wars worldwide.

A. nuclear   B. propaganda   C. proxy

1.

Answers:

1. America and The Soviets avoided outright military conflict in _____ for the duration of the Cold War.

C. Europe

2. The U.S. made a prolonged (1964–1975) and fruitless attempt to stop communist ______ from annexing South Vietnam.

B. North Vietnam

3. But in the late 1980s, under __________'s leadership, the Cold War started to disintegrate.

A. Mikhail S. Gorbachev

4. Another significant factor in the Cold War disintegration was U.S. President __________.

B. Richard Nixon

5. The Soviet Union and the United States backed several _______ wars worldwide.

C. proxy

1.

SOVIET UNION: THE DOWNFALL

The Guard Tower at the Berlin Wall. Nikita Khrushchev, the Soviet Union head, advised East Germany to block off passage between East and West Berlin to stop migration to the West.

Nikita Khrushchev envisioned the Soviet Union as a prosperous nation where the organization ruled democracy. However, a large number of conservatives in the Presidium party hindered him from being very revolutionary in the majority of policy matters. Presidium is the name for the permanent executive committee in a communist state. Stalin's legacy was destroyed by Khrushchev, who criticized his methods for governing the nation after 1934. He clearly said that intimidation would not be used in politics in the future.

A strong supporter of the communist ideal, Khrushchev tried to convert the entire world. He discussed socialist alternatives that Stalin had abandoned in 1948. While pursuing humanitarian socialism, he kept the Stalinist mechanisms in place. Stalinism is the term for Joseph Stalin's methods of governance or policies. It includes a Communist Party monopoly on authority, a centrally controlled economy, and government control of education, culture, and media.

Khrushchev started a ripple and influenced a protest writing that went beyond criticisms of Stalin to assault on the very principles of the Soviet regime. It captivated large sectors of the intellectuals and the young. The situation in Hungary reached a boiling point in October 1956 when Soviet troops had to violently put down a revolt organized by local communists that sought freedom from Moscow. In June 1957, a significant proportion of the Presidium addressed Khrushchev and requested that he vacate his position and take over as minister of agriculture. Khrushchev was eventually ousted from office. It is also widely accepted that the Soviet Union's disgrace in Cuba during the missile crisis significantly influenced Khrushchev's removal from power in October 1964.

Overall, Khrushchev was advantageous for the U.S.S.R. and the rest of the globe. He started the democratic transition, which Brezhnev suspended, but Gorbachev continued. America and the U.S.S.R. formed a more cordial relationship. In the former Soviet Union, democratic revolutions were brewing while the country suffered political and economic instability. Progress was also delayed due to the economic downturn.

One group of conservative reformers that gained notoriety included Mikhail Gorbachev. Gorbachev was upfront about his policy choices when he assumed office in March 1985. He emphasized the need for more social equality, a more significant responsibility for local soviets, and increased worker involvement in the enterprise. Gorbachev intended to start a top-down directed revolution. He proposed two sets of laws that he anticipated would change the country's political structure and make the U.S.S.R. a wealthier, more productive nation. These measures were known as perestroika and glasnost.

The glasnost program of Gorbachev aimed for political transparency. It discussed the personal limitations faced by Soviet citizens. Gorbachev's strategy for economic reconstruction was known as perestroika. The Soviet Union started transitioning under perestroika toward a diverse communist-capitalist society similar to contemporary China. The control of the economy would remain under the supervision of the Politburo, the Communist Party's decision-making body.

The Communist Party leadership swiftly grew rich and powerful in the 1960s and 1970s while millions of ordinary Soviet residents went hungry. Food and other consumer products were frequently in limited supply due to the Soviet Union's aggressive industrialization efforts. People in the Soviet Union often lacked access to necessities like shoes and clothing. Younger people reacted negatively to the gap between the enormous wealth of the Politburo and the deprivation of Soviet people. Unlike their parents, they resisted embracing the Communist Party's philosophy.

Additionally, the Soviet economy came under threat from

outside forces. During President Ronald Reagan's regime, the Soviet economy was cut off from the world in the 1980s. He also played a role in lowering oil prices to levels not seen in decades. The Soviet Union started to lose control over Eastern Europe when its gas and oil revenues plummeted.

Gorbachev's initiatives, however, were delayed from taking effect and contributed more to the Soviet Union's demise than to its preservation. The Berlin Wall was brought down due to the 1989 political uprising in Poland. This rebellion spawned further, generally peaceful revolts in other Eastern European nations. Towards the end of 1989, the U.S.S.R. had disintegrated entirely. Gorbachev handed in his resignation as U.S.S.R. president on December 25. On December 31, 1991, the Soviet Union disintegrated.

Fun Fact: *Race to Space.*

In a Space Race that lasted for 20 years, the two superpowers also competed to demonstrate technological superiority. The first artificial satellite, Sputnik-1, was launched by the Soviet Union in 1957. In 1969, the US became the first to dispatch a man to the moon. The two countries started working on joint missions in the middle of the 1970s.

Fun Fact: *The Most Fatal Proxy War.*

The Vietnam War was the bloodiest proxy war throughout the Cold War. It lasted from November 1955 to April 1975. North and South Vietnam fought each other in the conflict. Notably, the Soviet Union and China were allies of North Vietnam, whereas the United States of America supported South Vietnam. There were nearly 3.5 million casualties.

Trivia Questions:

1. Who envisioned the Soviet Union as a prosperous nation where the organization ruled democracy?

2. What did Khrushchev start that was advantageous for the U.S.S.R. and the rest of the globe?

3. What was the most fatal proxy war?

4. When did the U.S.S.R. disintegrate?

5. In the Space Race, what was America's milestone in 1969?

Answers:

1. Who envisioned the Soviet Union as a prosperous nation where the organization ruled democracy? **Nikita Khrushchev**

2. What did Khrushchev start that was advantageous for the U.S.S.R. and the rest of the globe? **Democratic transition**

3. What was the most fatal proxy war? **Vietnam War**

4. When did the U.S.S.R. disintegrate? **Towards the end of 1989**

5. In the Space Race, what was America's milestone in 1969? **The first to dispatch a man to the moon.**

THE COLD WAR INFLUENCE ON TODAY'S WORLD

In 1991, the Soviet Union fell apart, giving birth to 15 new self-governing countries, including a democratic anti-communist government in Russia. In an address at Berlin's Brandenburg Gate two years prior, President Reagan had urged Gorbachev to break the wall down. The Berlin Wall, which had served as the Cold War's most prominent icon for years, was finally taken down in November 1989. The Cold War was finally over. However, what does this all signify at this point?

The world situation was altered by the Cold War's conclusion in 1989 and the subsequent disintegration of the Soviet Union. Fundamentally, there was only one powerhouse left: the United States. As a result, the Cold War basis for foreign military involvement was eliminated. Still, new justifications for them began to emerge. The Gulf War versus Iraq in 1991, which required more than 500,000 U.S. soldiers to defend the commercial world's oil resources, was the most significant foreign mission.

The reasons behind the other actions, however, were very diverse. In Somalia, where there were no apparent U.S. interests at risk, the objective was to eliminate any barriers to providing food for a population dying of hunger. Armed forces were stationed in Kosovo and Bosnia, where Serbia was the target of a bombing campaign. It was carried out to prevent the cultural slaughter and the start of a regional conflict. Others viewed America as a worldwide tyrant, while others saw it as the world's police force. Nobody, however, could dispute the nation's substantial power and impact felt almost everywhere in the world.

Historians often regard the Cold War as a pivotal period in the chaotic history of the twentieth century. However, analysts are less in agreement about the bipolar conflict's importance now. Three components make up the actual legacy of the Cold War. First, nuclear weapons and the associated defense cuts and arms control agreements. Local disputes that have long-term effects come in second, followed by international organizations, which still play a significant role in today's world. The two leading organizations overseeing the "West," NATO and the European Union (E.U.), have origins in the bipolar period. The sense of belonging, solidarity and shared values that distinguish them were developed over many years.

The continuous existence of transatlantic institutions like NATO and the European Union and specific challenges like nuclear weapons and unpleasant regional conflicts demonstrate the Cold War's continuing importance. The transatlantic relationship was established, reinforced, and developed when the U.S. and the European nations perceived a similar threat. Many had expected that NATO would be dismantled after the Cold War. However, the alliance stayed in force and accepted new members, increasing its membership to include many former rivals from the disintegrated Warsaw Pact.

By 1990, the Cold War was over, but economic development and a generally growing standard of living have persisted. Political democracy also has advanced. However, the minor decline from 90 "free" countries in 2012 to 88 in 2013 serves as a reminder that individual liberty, democratic elections, and the legal system are delicate accomplishments that are quickly destroyed.

Fun Fact:

We have the Cold War to thank for the internet. The Cold War gave rise to the world wide web. Defense Advanced Research Projects Agency (ARPA), a program created by the US government, was created to find a fast way for military computers to exchange data. This served as the very first step toward the modern internet.

Fun Fact: *Playing spy.*

Both nations engaged in intensive spying on one another. The Central Intelligence Agency (CIA) exists in the United States. The Committee for State Security (KGB) exists in the Soviet Union. The CIA and American magician John Mulholland collaborated in the 1950s to create a book of tricks that CIA agents could utilize. The techniques included trickery, suggestions for how to dress to fit in, and strategies for sending hidden messages.

Discussion Questions:

The world situation was altered by the conclusion of the Cold War in 1989 and the following disintegration of the Soviet Union. Fundamentally, there was only one powerhouse left: the United States. As a result, the Cold War basis for foreign military involvement was eliminated, but new justifications for them began to emerge. The Gulf War versus Iraq in 1991, which required more than 500,000 U.S. soldiers to defend the commercial world's oil resources, was by far the biggest foreign mission. U.S. military involvement continued in Somalia, Kosovo, and Bosnia even after the Cold War. The reasons behind these actions were very diverse. Others viewed America as a worldwide bully, while others saw it as the world's police force.

Personal Reflections: **What do you think about America's military involvement even after the Cold War? Is America a bully? Why or why not?**

CONCLUSION

"Peace is not unity in similarity but unity in diversity, in the comparison and conciliation of differences."

- Mikhail S. Gorbachev

The term "Cold War" is utilized because the two superpowers did not engage in extensive direct combat. However, they supported opposing parties in significant regional "proxy wars." The two powerhouses were utilizing the world as a chessboard during the conflict. Similar to other disputes, both parties believed their positions were worth fighting for. Therefore, it's impossible to cast the blame on anyone.

Despite not being an armed war, the Cold War still resulted in millions of fatalities. The Soviet Union and America engaged in proxy wars that resulted in these deaths. The question of whether anything positive came from the four decades-long battle may be raised. In truth, there have been several debates among journalists, historians, and political analysts on how to understand the nature and causes of the conflict.

From an anticommunist viewpoint, the US-led alliance's persistence and perseverance in opposing Soviet and Soviet-influenced territorial expansion embodied the core of the Cold War. This contributed to the other two crucial developments, making them possible. First is global economic expansion, and second is political reform. According to economists, the global economic expansion has substantially enhanced foreign travel and improved overall wealth and average per capita earnings. It has also improved people's capacity to buy cars, computers, cell phones, and other consumer goods in several nations worldwide. The second factor is political reform, which, according to the reputable nonprofit organization Freedom House, has increased the number of "free" countries worldwide from 41 in 1975 to 90 in 2012.

It is also significant to note that during the 1962 Cuban Missile Crisis, the two superpowers came uncomfortably close to a nuclear war. Thankfully, Washington and Moscow began the first atomic arms talks to lessen the likelihood of nuclear conflict in the future. The Cold War, unfortunately, may have demonstrated that the two global powerhouses hold the entire planet in their hands. However, they have also shown that negotiations for peace are feasible.

BIBLIOGRAPHY

1. Britannica, The Editors of Encyclopaedia. Cold War. (30 November 2022). Encyclopedia Britannica. https://www.britannica.com/event/Cold-War.

2. Britannica, The Editors of Encyclopaedia. Marshall Plan. (24 November 2022). https://www.britannica.com/event/Marshall-Plan.

3. Britannica, The Editors of Encyclopaedia. Warsaw Pact. (23 December 2022). https://www.britannica.com/event/Warsaw-Pact.

4. Conquest, R., McCauley, M., Pipes, R.E., and Dewdney, J.C. Soviet Union. (18 October 2022). Encyclopedia Britannica. https://www.britannica.com/place/Soviet-Union.

5. History.com Editors. Cold War History. (12 January 2023). https://www.history.com/topics/cold-war/cold-war-history.

6. History.com Editors. Potsdam Conference Concludes. (30 July 2020). https://www.history.com/this-day-in-history/potsdam-conference-concludes.

7. History.com Editors. Soviet Union. (11 January 2023). https://www.history.com/topics/european-history/history-of-the-soviet-union.

8. Levering, R.B. The Cold War. (2016). West Sussex, United Kingdom. John Wiley and Sons, Inc., 2016.

9. Llewellyn, J. and Thompson, S. The Cold War Alliances. (16 September 2020). Alpha History. https://alphahistory.com/coldwar/cold-war-alliances/.

10. North Atlantic Treaty Organization. A Short History of NATO. (03 June 2022). https://www.nato.int/cps/en/natohq/declassified_139339.htm.

11. Student Center, Encyclopaedia Britannica. Cold War Alliances

and Leaders. (n.d.)

https://www.britannica.com/study/cold-war-alliances-and-leaders.

Image License-Free

1. A photo of President Franklin D. Roosevelt in his hometown, Hyde Park, New York, in 1943. The Great Depression, World War II, and the start of the Cold War all occurred during his term in office.

   "Public Domain: Franklin D. Roosevelt in Hyde Park, New York, 1943 (NARA)" by pingnews.com is marked with Public Domain Mark 1.0. To view the terms, visit https://creativecommons.org/publicdomain/mark/1.0//?ref= openverse.

2. A photo of Joseph Stalin and his children. From the middle of the 20th century until his death in 1953, Joseph Stalin presided over the Soviet Union.

   "What Happened To Joseph Stalin's Children" by manhhai is licensed under CC BY 2.0. To view a copy of this license, visit https://creativecommons.org/licenses/by/2.0/?ref=openverse.

3. (From Left to Right) Picture of Joseph Stalin, Franklin Roosevelt, and Winston Churchill on the porch of the Russian Embassy. The photo was taken during the Tehran Conference in 1943.

   "No Known Restrictions: President Roosevelt at Tehran Conference, 1943 (LOC)" by pingnews.com is marked with Public Domain Mark 1.0. To view the terms, visit https://creativecommons.org/publicdomain/mark/1.0/?ref= openverse.

4. Robert Schuman, the foreign minister of France, helps ratify the North Atlantic Treaty. The image was taken in Washington, D.C., at a formal ceremony to establish the North Atlantic Treaty Organization (NATO) on April 4, 1949. "NATO-CREATION-SCHUMAN-" by Patochka is licensed under CC BY 2.0. To view a copy of this license, visit https://creativecommons.org/licenses/by/2.0/?ref=openverse.

5. The Guard Tower at the Berlin Wall. Nikita Khrushchev, the Soviet Union head, advised East Germany to block off passage between East and West Berlin to stop migration to the West. "Guard Tower Berlin Wall" by popo.uw23 is marked with Public Domain Mark 1.0. To view the terms, visit https://creativecommons.org/publicdomain/mark/1.0//?ref= openverse.

6. A photo of Hiroshima, Japan which was completely destroyed by the atomic bomb on August 6, 1945, at precisely 8:15 a.m. The Hiroshima Prefectural Industrial Promotion Hall is the structure that is still partly surviving. "Hiroshima-after-the-bomb" by Maarten1979 is licensed under CC BY-SA 2.0. To view a copy of this license, visit https://creativecommons.org/licenses/by-sa/2.0/?ref=openverse.

7. Aerial photos of Nagasaki, Japan before (left) and after the (right) bombing in August 1945. The bombings at Hiroshima and Nagasaki prompted Japan's surrender. (Before) "Aerial view of Nagasaki before the bombing" by The Official CTBTO Photostream is licensed under CC BY 2.0. To view a copy of this license, visit https://creativecommons.org/licenses/by/2.0/?ref=openverse (After) "Aerial view of Nagasaki after the bombing" by The Official CTBTO Photostream is licensed under CC BY 2.0. To

view a copy of this license, visit

8. The Soviet Union leader, Nikita Khrushchev, with U.S. President John F. Kennedy in Vienna, in 1961. Khrushchev successfully mediated talks with the US to ease Cold War hostility.

   "Public Domain: Kennedy and Khrushchev in Vienna by Stanley Tretick, 1961 (NARA)" by pingnews.com is marked with Public Domain Mark 1.0. To view the terms, visit

9. Mikhail Gorbachev was the final ruler of the U.S.S.R. He introduced economic transformation that destroyed institutions that depended on nationalized commodities and opened his nation to the West.

   "Mikhail Gorbachev" by veni markovski is licensed under CC BY 2.0. To view a copy of this license, visit

About Us

At our core, we believe that history is more than just a subject to be learned. It's an experience to be had.

Our mission is to educate and inspire the next generation by providing them with a window into the fascinating and often surprising world of the past. We want to help young people make sense of the complexities of history and understand the lessons it has to offer.

By creating unforgettable encounters with relics of the past, we hope to ignite a lifelong passion for learning and discovery.

Thank you,